abraham lincoln

The Practical Mystic

francis grierson

Originally Published in 1918

TABLE OF CONTENTS

The Practical Mysticism of Abraham Lincoln

The Divine Will

The Mystical Awakening

The Agnostic and the Mystic

The Logic of the Supernatural

The Mystical Mood

"Going into the Silence"

Invisible Powers

The Fusion of Spirit and Matter

His Miraculous Progress

A Prophetic Witness

Lincoln's Simplicity

Lincoln's Clairvoyant Wit

A Prophetic Vision of Hades

Shakespeare and Lincoln

A Prophecy Fulfilled

The Ordinances of Heaven

Lincoln's Face

The Great Debate

Forecasting and Premonitions

Illumination of the Spirit

Tycho Brahe and Lincoln

Herndon's Analysis and Testimony

An Original Mind

The Great Books

Veneration and Truth

The Great Puzzle

Lincoln's Energy and Will

Nature and Prophecy

The Seal of Nature

Law and Authority

Lincoln as Critic

His Style

Lincoln's Serenity

The Romance of His Character

President by the Grace of God

Science and the Mystical

The Old and the New

Destiny versus Will

James Jacquess Practical Mystic

Images and Dreams

The New Era

The Practical Mysticism of Abraham Lincoln

A knowledge of the influences which ruled the life of Lincoln, the greatest of practical mystics, is essential now that a new form of paganism and slavery threatens humanity.

In Lincoln's time the black slaves of America had to be freed; in our time the white slaves of Europe have to be freed. We have returned to the conquest. History is being repeated, but on a far vaster scale. The whole world is groaning under the threats and deeds of tyranny that seeks to become absolute. What Abraham Lincoln stood for in the middle of the nineteenth century the English-speaking peoples must stand for at the beginning of the twentieth. Materialism produced Prussian autocracy. A spiritual power brought America safely through the ordeals of the Civil War. But the material and the spiritual cannot both rule at the same time. One must yield authority to the other. And we cannot succeed by denying the very thing which caused Lincoln to triumph over all enemies and obstacles.

In 1862 the Reverend Byron Sutherland went with some friends of the President to call upon him. On November 15th, 1872, Dr. Sutherland wrote to the Reverend J. A. Reed:—

"The President began by saying, 'The ways of God are mysterious and profound beyond all comprehension. "Who, by searching, can find Him out?" Now, judging after the manner of men, taking counsel of our sympathies and feelings, if it had been left to us to determine it, we would have had no war. And, going farther back, to the occasion of it, we would have had no evil. There is the mystery of the universe which no man can solve, and it is at that point that human understanding backs down. There is nothing left but for the heart of man to take up faith and believe where it cannot reason. Now, I believe we are all agents and instruments of Divine Providence. On both sides we are working out the will of God. Yet how strange the spectacle! Here is one half of the nation prostrated in prayer that God will help to destroy the Union and build up a government upon the corner-stone of human bondage. And here is the other half, equally earnest in their prayers and efforts to defeat a purpose which they regard as so repugnant to their ideas of human nature and the rights of society, as well as liberty and independence. They want slavery; we want freedom. They want a servile class; we want to make equality practicable as far as possible. And they are Christians and we are Christians. They and we are praying and fighting for results exactly the opposite. What must God think of such a posture of affairs? There is but one solution—self-deception. Somewhere there is a fearful heresy in our religion, and I cannot think it lies in the love of liberty and in the aspirations of the human soul. I hold myself in my present position, and with the authority invested in me, as an instrument of Providence. I have my own views and purposes. I have my convictions of duty and my ideas of what is right to be done. But I am conscious every moment that all I am, and all I have, is subject to the control of a Higher Power. Nevertheless, I am no fatalist. I believe in the supremacy of the human conscience, and that men are responsible beings; that God has a right to hold them—and will hold them—to a strict personal account for the deeds done in the body.... God alone knows the issue of this business. He has destroyed nations from the map of history for their sins. Nevertheless, my hopes prevail generally above my fears for our Republic. The times are dark. The spirits of ruin are abroad in all their power and the mercy of God alone can save us.'"

Francis Grierson

The Divine Will

September 30th, 1862, when everything looked dark and the future of America was uncertain, Lincoln wrote the following meditation on the Divine Will:—

"The will of God prevails. In great contests each party claims to act in accordance with the will of God. Both may be, one must be, wrong. God cannot be for and against the same thing at the same time. In the present civil war it is quite possible that God's purpose is something different from the purpose of either party; and yet the human instrumentalities, working just as they do, are of the best adaptation to affect His purpose. I am almost ready to say this is probably true: that God wills this contest, and wills that it shall not end yet. By His great power on the minds of the contestants he could have either saved or destroyed the Union without war. Yet the contest began. And, having begun, He could give the final victory to either side any day. Yet the contest proceeds."

Francis Grierson

The Mystical Awakening

A mystical epoch is upon us, and like all vital movements it has come without systematic propaganda and without organised effort.

The world-upheaval did not cause this new movement; it has simply advanced it by stripping materialism of its illusive trappings and showing it naked to the civilised world. It is not the work of one man or any single group, sect, or nation. Its characteristics are Anglo-American, and its development will prove the only antidote to the new pagan Kultur, which opposes not only Christian morals but everything that places the spiritual above the material.

Abraham Lincoln, the greatest practical mystic the world has known for nineteen hundred years, is the one man whose life and example ought to be clearly set before the English-speaking peoples at this supreme climax in the history of civilisation. The thoughts, incidents, manifestations, which the majority of historians glide over with a careless touch, or sidetrack because of the lack of moral courage, are the only things that count in the life of that great seer. His whole existence was controlled by influences beyond the ken of the most astute politicians of his time. His genius was superhuman. And since this world is not governed by chance, a power was at work which fore-ordained him for his unique mission.

W. H. Herndon has this to say in his biography of the immortal statesman:—

"Nature had burned into him her holy fire and stamped him with the seal of her greatness."

In other words, the seal of the practical mystic, which may be taken as the keynote to the spiritual theme of his marvellous experiences. For it is futile to continue to harp on Lincoln's political acumen, his knowledge of law, his understanding of the people, his judgment of individuals, his poverty, his disregard of the conventional, as causes of his greatness. The same may be said of thousands of others, yet there is no other Lincoln. To arrive at a just appreciation of the man and his achievements I felt it essential to read very carefully all the books written by those most intimate with the great President—a study which has required a period of thirty years. The writing of "The Valley of Shadows" was one of the results of that study, that book being, as far as I could make it, a depiction of the spiritual atmosphere of the Lincoln country in Lincoln's time—the atmosphere in which he lived and moved, thought and worked.

Too long has the materialism of weights and bushel measures dimmed the light that shines from the example of that incomparable seer. Too long have politicians used his name to fish for gudgeons in the muddy waters of sectional politics. Too long has Lincoln been held up in speeches and electioneering manœuvres as a politician who arrived because he was honest. As if Webster, Calhoun, Clay, Sumner, and scores of others were not equally honest without ever attaining a world-influence. What caused Lincoln's honesty? His conscience. And what created his conscience? His innate mystical knowledge of the difference between good and evil, philosophers and puppets, the solemn dignity of duty and the sham dignity of ambition. His was the clear vision in the darkest hours while others were magnifying events through long-distance spectacles, or minimising them in near-sighted details.

The mystical trend now visible in England and America is not a revival but a renaissance. It has come in the natural course of events, being the only thing that responds to the spiritual aspirations and needs of the dispensation ushered in by the great war.

The renaissance of practical mysticism is now apparent both in and outside the churches; but its greatest influence is exerted on that large class which, before the war, had no religious convictions of any kind. We have arrived at a climax in history. Old methods and systems are passing, but not the old fundamental truths. Conditions, not principles, have changed, and our attitude towards things has changed with conditions. Thousands can now see clearly where once they saw through a veil of agnosticism. It required a mighty force to lift the veil, and a vast amount of machinery and metaphysics had to combine to accomplish such a miracle; but the miracle is here, alive with a vital flame unknown since the days of the Prophets and the Apostles.

The spiritual renaissance is not a drawing-room fad. It is not founded on a passing whim. Novelties and opinions shift with the wind, and people who are influenced by them are influenced by shadows. Mere notions can never take the place of ideas. Novelties possess no fundamental basis on which the spirit of man can build, and the difference between an idea and a notion is the difference between a university and a lunatic asylum.

The spiritual renaissance is not confined to any particular profession, and this is why it is making headway among people of such divers views. The war has crushed the juice out of the orange on the tree of pleasure and nothing is left but the peel over which materialism is slipping to its doom.

This stupendous movement was not sprung upon the world in a night. It has had its slow stages of development. Everything comes and goes in cycles which are graded in kind and proceed in accordance with immutable law. This spiritual movement has had its special phases of preparation. It is not true that the voices of the prophets have been inaudible. What is true is that every voice that has sounded since the dawn of historical civilisation has been heard and heeded. Emerson uttered a great mystical truth when he said: "A book written for three will gravitate to three," and, similarly, a voice intended for three will be heard and heeded by three.

Francis Grierson

The Agnostic and the Mystic

Herndon's agnosticism left no lasting impression on the mind of Lincoln. This is remarkable, because Herndon was a man with a powerful originality and a strong will.

Lincoln was more or less influenced by Herndon at the beginning of their acquaintance but such influence did not last long.

Another curious thing is that Mr. Herndon, in spite of his probity, his practical ability, and his talent as a lawyer, never became known beyond his own state. He never was put forward as a leader. Perhaps he entertained no particular ambition to lead, being too much of a philosopher, but the remark is in order that what was lacking in his temperament was just a spark of that mystical illumination which gave Lincoln his faith, his conviction, and his power.

No doubt Herndon was singularly fitted for the position he held with Lincoln for the space of twenty years. Had he been a leader in public affairs he could not have aided Lincoln as he did.

That the great President never had a mentor is plain to all who have studied the best biographies. He did sometimes act upon suggestions from friends in matters of minor importance in his private affairs. When, one day, after he had become President, Mrs. Lincoln informed him that the gossips declared he was being ruled by Seward, his reply was: "I may not rule myself out, certainly Seward shall not. The only ruler is my conscience—following God in it—and these men will have to learn that yet." And Seward did learn it, as well as Stanton and Chase, and every member of the Cabinet, and all others who came within the radius of his mystical circuit. Indeed, the generals all learnt it, some of them to their sorrow, long before the war ended.

Lincoln's authority became apparent to all whenever he delivered a speech on important occasions. Then, as Judge Whitney has said, he was "as terrible as an army with banners." Col. Henry Watterson, in his memorable address before the Lincoln Union, in Chicago, puts the question: "Where did Shakespeare get his genius? Where did Mozart get his music? Whose hand smote the lyre of the Scottish ploughman? God alone. And if Lincoln was not inspired of God then there is no such thing as special Providence or the interposition of Divine Power in the affairs of men."

The Logic of the Supernatural

Judge Henry C. Whitney has asked the following questions:—
"By what magic spell was this, the greatest moral transformation in all profane history, wrought? What Genius sought out this roving child of the forest, this obscure flatboatman, and placed him on the lonely heights of immortal fame? Why was this best of men made the chief propitiation for our national sins? Was his progress causative or fortuitous; was it logical or supernatural; was the Unseen Power, or he himself, the architect of his fortune?

"The blunders that were committed by raw and reckless commanders in the field were sufficient to make angels weep, but they were all mosaics in the process of Fate to work out the Divine plan. If we could see the whole scheme of human redemption it would be quite clear to us that not only Abraham Lincoln, U. S. Grant, W. T. Sherman, but equally Jefferson Davis, Robert E. Lee, Stonewall Jackson, and Raphael Semmes were necessary instruments of the great disposer of events—that the bullet which terminated the glorious career of the President was not more surely sped by Fate to its mark than was the bullet which ended the life of Albert Sidney Johnston at Shiloh and which ultimately averted ruin to the Union forces on that blood-stained field, and that in the sublime procession of destiny all events, apparent accidents, calamities, crimes, and blunders were agents of the omnipotent will, now as cause, then as interlude or eddy, anon as effort, all working, apparently, and to human comprehension, fortuitously, but in reality all harmoniously to their Divine appointed end."

The Mystical Mood

"There was to me," says Henry B. Rankin, in his "Personal Recollections of Abraham Lincoln," "always an unapproachable grandeur in the man when he was in this mood of inner solitude. It isolated and—I always thought—exalted him above his ordinary life. History will discern and reverently disclose the strength in Lincoln's character and the executive foresight for which this mood gave him revealings."

And the Reverend Joseph Fort Newton adds to the sentiments of his friend Rankin these words: "Lincoln was a man whom to know was a kind of religion. His deep musings on the ways of God, on the souls of men, on the principles of justice and the laws of liberty bore fruit in exalted character and exact insight. Hence, a style of speech remarkable for its lucidity, direction, and forthright power, with no waste of words, tinged always by a temperament at once elusive and alluring, which Bryce compares to the weighty eloquence of Cromwell without its haziness."

Francis Grierson

"Going into the Silence"

During an important criminal trial Amzi McWilliams said: "Lincoln will pitch in heavy now for he has hid."

One who knew him declared: "He seemed never to be alone. I have frequently seen him, in the midst of a Court in session, with his mind completely withdrawn from the busy scene before his eyes, as completely abstracted as if he were in absolute solitude."

Judge Whitney wrote: "In religion, Lincoln was in essence a mystic, and all his adoration was in accordance with the tenets of that order," a judgment which agrees with that of Alexander H. Stephens, Vice President of the Southern Confederacy: "With Lincoln, the Union rose to the sublimity of a religious Mysticism."

The mystical mood cannot be likened to any other mood. People in a hurry never experience such a mental state. Personal ambition forbids it and the feeling of vainglory renders such a condition impossible. What renders the life of Lincoln so instructive is the fact that with him everything was so natural. He did not experiment; he did not practise special hours and seasons; he had no fixed times for this or that. He professed no subtle methods of inducing moods and took no stimulants. Nature and a mystical Providence arranged and provided.

His moods were between himself and his God. No one ever dared approach him as to the why or the wherefore of his silence. And it is proper here to comment on the instinctive good sense of the American people in whose midst Lincoln passed his whole life—they instinctively knew too much to presume upon the privacy of his mystical moods. In this their attitude was wholly admirable. The American people were at that time practical, democratic seers, without whom the greatest practical mystic could not have existed.

That Lincoln possessed intuition and illumination without resorting to human aid is clear and irrefutable. His words were simple and his actions were simple, like those of the Hebrew seers. He announced and he pronounced, without subtle explanations or mysterious formulas.

All which proves that practical mysticism can nourish as much under a Democracy as under any other form of government.

Men do not receive their gifts from those in power. They come into the world with them. Lincoln was opposed on all sides from the start. He had to contend with poverty, provincial ignorance, aristocratic prejudice, academical opposition, and he had against him his homely features, his awkward bearing, and the lack of influential patronage. He had no family connections that could be of assistance anywhere at any time. Never had there been a man of great intellect so absolutely alone in the intellectual world, so removed from social and political favours of time and circumstance.

Francis Grierson

Invisible Powers

We are compelled to look at all sides of Lincoln's political career in order to arrive at a just appreciation of his stupendous achievements, and when that is done we have to dismiss the notion that he succeeded because of his brilliant intellectual gifts. Others possessed great intellects without attaining altitudes of commanding power and enduring fame.

Why did the influence of Cæsar, Darius, Alexander, Bonaparte, and Bismarck cease as soon as they passed away? Because the influence they exerted was based on material dominion. With the collapse of the material everything collapses. The material can never go beyond or take precedence of the spiritual. Marcus Aurelius is read to-day because he placed spiritual things above all worldly possessions and privileges.

The universe was created by a Supreme Mind and the direction of affairs is in the hands of this All-Seeing Power, manifesting in all forms—sometimes personal, sometimes collective. In Lincoln's case it took a pronounced individual form, isolated and unique, as in Moses. The ease with which Lincoln overcame opposition amazed those who were near him. They judged it miraculous. Miracles are manifestations for which science has no definition, no analysis. Lincoln's intelligence was not bound by the known rules and laws of science. It requires intuition and illumination for its realisation. Such intelligence cannot be handled in detail as chemists handle the elements of matter. In the mystical world all the elements, forces, and combinations act and develop together as one manifestation at one time. No mental chemistry can separate them.

The Fusion of Spirit and Matter

"The existence of a great man," says Victor Cousin, the French philosopher, "is not the creation of arbitrary choice; he is not a thing that may, or may not, exist; he is not merely an individual; too much, or too little, of individuality are equally destructive to the character of a great man. On the one hand, individuality of itself is an element of what is pitiful and little, because particularity, the contingent and the finite, tends unceasingly to division, to dissolution, and to nothingness. On the other hand, every general tends to absolute unity. It possesses greatness but it is exposed to the risk of losing itself in abstractions. The great man is the harmonious combination of what is particular with what is general. This combination constitutes the standard value of his greatness, and it involves a two-fold condition: first, of representing the general spirit of his nation, because it is in his relation to that general spirit that his greatness consists; and, secondly, of representing the general spirit which confers upon his greatness in his own person, in a real form, that is, in a finite, positive, visible, and determinate form; so that what is general may not suppress what is particular; and that which is particular may not dissipate and dissolve what is general—that the infinite and the finite may be blended together in that proportion which truly constitutes human greatness."

All which applies to Lincoln.

"Conceive a great machine," wrote Guizot, the historian, "the design of which is centred in a single mind, though its various parts are entrusted to various workmen, separated from, and strangers to, each other. No one of them understands the work as a whole, nor the general result which he concerts in producing; but every one executes with intelligence and freedom, by rational and voluntary acts, the particular task assigned to him. It is thus that by the hand of man the designs of Providence are wrought out in the government of the world. It is thus that the two great facts, which are apparent in the history of civilisation, come to co-exist. On the one hand, those portions of it which may be considered as fated, or which happen without the control of human knowledge or will; on the other hand, the part played in it by the freedom and intelligence of man and what he contributes to it by means of his own knowledge and will."

His Miraculous Progress

One of the most searching biographers of Lincoln maintains that between the ages of fourteen and twenty-eight he displayed no sign of embryonic or assured greatness.

If this be true, it means that none of Lincoln's early friends were intuitive enough to discover his greatness. Even the best writers who have dealt with this fascinating subject have failed to see all the facts, all the influences, all the correlated powers, in connection with what looks to many like a life of miracle. Intelligence and power are not attained by any mental hocus-pocus or metaphysics. Diamonds in the rough are still diamonds, or no one would think of having them polished. The same law works in nature as in human nature. The great man is born, but he is not born with all his faculties developed, and he, like others, must pass through stages of progressive development. There is not one law for genius and another for mere talent.

A distinguished writer says:—

"Lincoln achieved greatness, but can the genesis of the mystery be analysed?"

Certainly not by the ordinary process of ordinary philosophers and scientists. What all writers up to the present have failed to see is that Lincoln's powers were a combination of the normal-practical and the practical-supernatural. His supernaturalism was positive, mathematical, and absolute. The only things which Lincoln had to learn as he went were the modes of application. He had to learn system and method, as was natural, but the principle came into the world with him. Everything that is concrete appears simple. The various qualities and elements that produce what we call mental illumination are hidden from the crowd and even from those who most profess to understand.

Jesse Dubois wrote to Judge Whitney that "after having been intimately associated with Lincoln for twenty-five years I now find that I never knew him."

The great man had unconsciously deceived his friends because of his outward simplicity. And this outward freedom was backed by his simplicity of speech and direct logic. It was all too simple. They were fooled by the outward material because the inward mystical took that form. His friends liked the man and worked to elect him principally for that reason, and this is why they were astonished later on when the practical mystic rose clear above all systems of politics and all the accepted philosophies, and accomplished the miraculous. The impossible happened. The President had to go more than half way through the Civil War before the real Lincoln became manifest to observing critics.

Francis Grierson

A Prophetic Witness

In his book, "Life on the Circuit with Lincoln," Judge Whitney comments:—

"As early as 1856, independent of all contemporary opinion, I conceived the idea that Mr. Lincoln was a prodigy of intellectual and moral force. Others associated with us deemed him superlatively great, but still human. I went farther; my view was definite and pronounced, that Lincoln was ordained for a greater than a merely human mission, and I avowed this belief as early as that time.

"His character as a lawyer was controlled and moulded by his character as a man. He understood human nature thoroughly and was an expert in the cross-examination of witnesses. If a witness told the truth without evasion Lincoln was respectful and patronising to him, but he would score a perjured witness unmercifully. He took no notes but remembered everything quite as well as those who did so. I remember once we all, Court and lawyers, except Lincoln, insisted that a witness had sworn so-and-so, but it turned out that Lincoln was correct and that he recollected better than the united bench and bar. But with all his candour, there was a method and shrewdness which Leonard Swett well understood and which he has thus forcibly expressed: 'As the trial progressed, where most lawyers object, he would say he "reckoned" it would be fair to admit this in, or that; and sometimes when his adversary could not quite prove what Lincoln knew to be the truth, he would say he "reckoned" it would be fair to admit the truth to be so-and-so. When he did object to the Court, when he heard his objections answered, he would often say, "Well, I reckon I must be wrong."'

"He was wise as a serpent in the trial of a case, but I have got too many scars from his blows to certify that he was harmless as a dove. When the whole thing is unravelled the adversary begins to see that what he was so blandly giving away was simply what he couldn't get and keep. By giving away six points and carrying the seventh he carried his case, and, the whole case hanging on the seventh, he traded everything which would give him the least aid in carrying that. Any one who took Lincoln for a simple-minded man would very soon wake up on his back, in a ditch."

Lincoln's Simplicity

There are two kinds of simplicity—one is without reason or discrimination, that believes all that is seen and heard if presented under the guise of honesty; the other is the kind that penetrates beneath manner, dress, verbiage, and meets all subterfuge, artifice, and sophistry with statements and facts at once logical and irrefutable. Lincoln was the most simple man in dress, in speech, in manners, in looks, that ever stood before the world in so great a rôle, but his intellect was anything but simple. He was never deceived by cunning devices and cunning manœuvres. Bacon has an essay showing the difference between cunning and wisdom, and it may be said that Lincoln's knowledge took the form of wisdom as distinguished from cunning. His management of a law case was that of a seer. The points he made were not made for personal gratification but for love of truth and justice. Not only he did not want to risk being deceived, he took every precaution to insure against deception. Here is where his welding of reason and logic produced in his marvellous intellect a kind of clairvoyance which his friends at the bar felt but could not analyse. The combination was unheard of! The lawyers and the judges could only reason from their own experience, they could only cite examples in their own lives, and this man Lincoln was unlike all that had been and all that was.

Lincoln's simplicity seemed to the casual observer of a character so trusting and so naïf that it deceived all the members of his Cabinet during the first two years of the war. They were used to smart men, clever men, academical men. They called for the routine of respectability and official dignity. To their minds the President seemed pliable and willing, and they set about instructing him in the a, b, c of high politics and the first principles of statesmanship. The President was in no way frustrated. He understood them in advance, having weighed them in the balance of his own judgment. He had found them honest but inexperienced, sincere but saucy. He knew they were living in an atmosphere of low visibility. At the proper moment he would turn on the searchlights and give them their bearings. Some of them expected to act as the President's pilot, while others expected to be captain of the ship-of-state with the President as pilot.

It took them more than two years to find out that this pioneer of the West was captain, pilot, and master of charts on a political sea the like of which they little dreamed existed. In one sense, he wore out their obstinacy by his patience. In another, he awaited opportunities to attest their errors and show his judgment, but matters proceeded with such calm that they could not understand with what power he acted, with what prescience he divined.

What mystified them was the combination of the practical with the spiritual, the clear vision with the maxims of ordinary business affairs, the penetration of the future while working in seeming darkness.

Francis Grierson

Lincoln's Clairvoyant Wit

Lincoln was not deceived by an outward show of religion. A Southern woman begged the President to have her husband released from a Northern prison, "for," she said, "although he is a Rebel he is a very religious man." Lincoln replied: "I am glad to hear that, because any man who wants to disrupt this Union needs all the religion in sight to save him."

He treated with indifference people who commandeered. A haughty woman came to Lincoln and demanded a colonel's commission for her son. "I demand it," she said, "not as a favour but as a right. Sir, my grandfather fought at Lexington, my father fought at New Orleans, and my husband was killed at Monterey."

"I guess, Madam," was Lincoln's reply, "your family has done enough for the country. It is time to give some one else a chance."

When Hugh McCullough, Secretary of the Treasury in Lincoln's second term, presented a delegation of New York bankers at the White House, McCullough said: "These gentlemen of New York have come on to see the Secretary of the Treasury about our new loan. As bankers, they are obliged to hold our national securities. I can vouch for their patriotism and loyalty, for, as the good Book says, 'Where the treasure is there will the heart be also.'"

To which Lincoln replied: "There is another text, Mr. McCullough, I remember, that might equally apply, 'Where the carcass is there will the eagles be gathered together.'"

Lincoln condemned as tedious a certain Greek history. When a diplomat present said: "The author of that history, Mr. President, is one of the profoundest scholars of the age; no one has plunged more deeply into the sacred fount of learning."

"Yes," replied Lincoln, "or come up drier."

When in Chicago in 1860, the mayor, John Wentworth, asked Lincoln why he did not get some astute politician to run him, Lincoln replied that "events and not a man's own exertions made presidents."

To Henry C. Whitney, Lincoln remarked: "Judd and Ray and those fellows think I don't see anything, but I see all around them. I see better what they want to do with me than they do themselves."

They were deceived, not by Lincoln, who never cared what individuals thought, but by Nature, which often sets a trap for people who live in a world of their own illusions. Nature, the medium through which the Divine mind manifests, is, so to speak, a mask through which egoists cannot penetrate and by which the cunning are led to destruction. Lincoln let them talk and even act, knowing that they themselves were the tools for their own undoing. While the ward politicians and others, who thought themselves far superior, laid their plans, schemed, and intrigued, the man of clear vision awaited unperturbed the events which he knew would put them all in their proper places. Little did they dream that they were mere incidents among the million of incidents that go to the making of one epoch-making event.

The practical mystic is little concerned with incidents. The multitude do not know in what direction they are going, moved and influenced as they are by the incidental, the accidental, the shifting illusions in which they live, but the man who knows why they are influenced also knows why he is influenced.

Lincoln was patient with the men who considered him a sort of political accident. He understood their point of view. He did not entertain feelings of revenge. Hundreds of men, like John Wentworth, are only mentioned to-day because of some passing incident which connected them with the man whom they regarded as a failure in politics.

A Prophetic Vision of Hades

That William Blake was a mystic of the practical kind there can be no question. In art and in poetry he had that illumination which Lincoln had in statesmanship.

The New York Times says:—

"That a century has failed to heap the dust of oblivion over England's 'Greatest Mystic,' William Blake, is exemplified by the reproduction in a recent issue of Country Life of one of Blake's engravings for Dante's Inferno, in which four fiends with cruel faces are torturing a soul in Hell."

The face of the chief devil, who is not actually engaged in the torture, but is an eager and interested spectator, might easily be taken for a portrait of the German Emperor. As suggested by W. F. Boudillon, the familiar, upturned moustachios must have puzzled Blake in his vision. He represented them as tusks growing from the corners of the mouth—it is to be noted that this fiend alone among the four has the tusks.

It is recorded of Blake, as a lad, that his father would have apprenticed him to Rylands, the Court Engraver—a man much liked and in great prosperity at the time—but Blake objected, saying: "Father, I do not like his face; he looks as if he would live to be hanged." Twelve years later Rylands committed forgery, and the prophecy came true.

Blake's visions, startling though they be, are not more startling than many prophecies made by Lincoln, as, for instance, his prophecy of prohibition, woman's rights, and the end of slavery, not to mention his visions concerning himself. The practical mystic sees through, the scientific materialist sees only, the surface. Eternity is the everlasting now. Blake drew a faithful portrait of the Kaiser Wilhelm II of Germany long before the Kaiser was born, and Tycho Brahe predicted the birth of a Swedish conqueror and what he would accomplish.

In these things there is no place for chance, nor is it true that the practical mystic is limited to poetry, or to art, or to music, or to religion, politics, and philosophy. Neither is the practical mystic confined to any particular social class or any creed.

Abraham Lincoln could not have directed affairs had he been a recluse. Before he became an adept in the direction of material affairs he had to be familiar with the practical ways of the world, and as a lawyer he passed through a school that left no place for vague theories or vain illusions. He frequently stripped others of their illusions, but being free of illusions himself he had none to lose. This made him invulnerable. His enemies were swayed by theories; nothing short of knowledge sufficed for this man, who reduced his adversaries to the position where they were kept constantly on the alert to know what manœuvre to employ next. They moved in a region of guess-work where there was no law except that of their own confusion and discomfiture.

Francis Grierson

Shakespeare and Lincoln

"Lincoln," says Judge Whitney, "was one of the most heterogeneous characters that ever played a part in the great drama of history, and it was for this reason that he was so greatly misjudged and misunderstood; that he was, on the one hand, described as a mere humourist—a sort of Artemus Ward or Mark Twain—that it was thought that, by some 'irony of Fate,' a low comedian had got into the Presidential chair, and that the nation was being delivered over to conflagration, while this modern Nero fiddled upon its ruins.

"One of his peculiarities was his inequality of conduct, his dignity, interspersed with freaks of frivolity and inanity; his high aspiration and achievement, and his descent into the most primitive vales of listlessness."

In the chief drawer of his cabinet table all the current joke books of the time were in juxtaposition with official commissions, lacking only the final signature, applications for pardons from death penalties, laws awaiting executive action, and orders which, when launched, would control the fate of a million men and the destinies of unborn generations. "Hence it was that superficial persons, who expected great achievements to be ushered in with a prologue, could not understand or appreciate that this great man's administration was a succession of acts of grand and heroic statesmanship, or that he was a prodigy of intellect and moral force."

The mystic Shakespeare and the mystic Lincoln have a connecting link in their wit and humour. Had Shakespeare left us only two dramas—Macbeth and Othello—no one would have dreamed of a creation like Falstaff emanating from the same mind, yet it is because of the union of the tragic and the humorous that Shakespeare is universally human, worldly wise as well as spiritual and metaphysical.

Shakespeare makes of the gravedigger in Hamlet a sort of clown with a spade, and throughout all his dramas wit and humour, pathos and tragedy, go hand in hand. Without his humour Shakespeare would have been little more than an English Racine. With Lincoln, humour was made to serve a high, psychic purpose. By its means he created a new atmosphere and new conditions through which he could all the more freely work and act. He brought humour into play for his own good as well as that of others. He was not a theorist, or a dreamer of dreams; he was a practical mystic.

A Prophecy Fulfilled

In a letter written from Springfield, Illinois, August 15th, 1855, to the Hon. George Robertson, of Lexington, Kentucky, Lincoln said:—

"The Autocrat of all the Russias will proclaim his subjects free sooner than will our American Masters voluntarily give up their slaves."

On the day before Lincoln's first inauguration as President of the United States the "Autocrat of all the Russias," Alexander the Second, by Imperial decree emancipated his serfs, while six weeks after the inauguration the "American Masters," headed by Jefferson Davis, began the great war of secession to perpetuate and spread the institution of slavery. This is only one of Lincoln's prophecies which proved true. In stating them he did not pass into an abnormal state. He spoke as one would speak of the coming weather. He did not consult the stars, nor any person, before making a prophetic statement. Seeing clearly was as natural to him as eating or sleeping. He was not a psychic machine, uttering thoughts which seemed strange and enigmatical to himself, because his intellectual and spiritual powers were part of himself.

Men of genius are not instruments in the vulgar meaning of the word. They do not act in ignorance of what they are doing and saying. Lincoln, more than any other, could give deliberate reasons for what he did and said, and it is exceedingly difficult to name another in history who was under such logical and commanding control of all the moral and intellectual faculties. When he seemed to the superficial observer to be dreaming, he was reasoning, calculating, comparing, analysing, weighing, turning things upside down and inside out, until he satisfied the dictates of his conscience and his sense of moral responsibility.

He placed no reliance on halfway measures and palliatives, no faith in the workings of chance. He therefore was not, and could never have been, a passive instrument in the hands of some unknown power. When it was said of a certain musician that he composed his operas under the direct influence of Mozart, the answer was: "Then who influenced Mozart?"

Great originality belongs to the mystical unity of the Supreme Intelligence. Had Lincoln imitated Henry Clay, whom he so much admired as a statesman and thinker, what would have become of Lincoln and the country he governed?

He who originates is authoritative, and, as Carlyle said, "All authority is mystical in its origin." In no single thing of importance did Lincoln copy any one's methods or systems. His trend of thought was at variance with the prevailing trend, even of those who were supposed to know the most.

Francis Grierson

The Ordinances of Heaven

"Canst thou bind the sweet influence of Pleiades, or loose the bands of Orion? Canst thou bring forth Mazzaroth in his season? Or canst thou guide Arcturus with his sons? Knowest thou the ordinances of heaven?"—Job.

Phenomena that arrive with the days, months, seasons, centuries, are accompanied by events of corresponding significance in the human world, for everything is related to everything else.

In 1858 a new party came into being, headed by the prophet from the wilderness, who was as much a phenomenon in the human world as the comet of that year was in the starry heavens—an apparition first observed by the Florentine astronomer, Donati. Some scientific authorities give Donati's comet an orbit of two thousand, others three thousand years. Its advent was as unexpected as was the advent of Lincoln. Its immense orbit, the splendour of its train, its seeming close proximity to the earth, the presentiments which it inspired in millions of the people, corresponded with the sentiments and sensations inspired by the phenomenal progress of Lincoln, the avatar of democratic freedom and justice. The following description is taken from "The Valley of Shadows":—

"After a long period of cloudy weather the sky cleared, and when darkness closed in the night came with a revelation. Never had such a night been witnessed by living man, for a great comet hung suspended in the shimmering vault like an immense silver arrow dominating the world and all the constellations. An unparalleled radiance illumined the prairie, the atmosphere vibrated with a strange, mysterious glow, and as the eye looked upward it seemed as if the earth was moving slowly towards the stars.

"The sky resembled a phantasmagoria seen from the summit of some far and fabulous Eden. The Milky Way spread across the zenith like a confluence of celestial altars flecked with myriads of gleaming tapers, and countless orbs rose out of the luminous veil like fleecy spires tipped with the blaze of opal and sapphire.

"The great stellar clusters appeared as beacons on the shores of infinite worlds, and night was the window from which the soul looked out on eternity."

Such was the celestial apparition that ushered in the new party which was to support Abraham Lincoln and send him to the White House.

In all vital phenomena there is periodicity. The barometer comes to its minimum height for the day between four and five in the evening; again, it is at its maximum height between eight and ten in the morning and between eight and ten in the evening. The two first of these periods is when the electric tension is at its minimum; at its maximum during the two latter periods. The basic unit of the lunar day is twelve hours. An ordinary or solar day is two days, and an ordinary week is two weeks. This hebdomadal or heptal cycle governs, either in its multiple or submultiple, an immense number of phenomena in animal life in which the number seven has a prominent place. A Mr. Hay, of Edinburgh, writing some sixty years ago, says:

"There is harmony of numbers in all nature—in the force of gravity, in the planetary movements, in the laws of heat, light, electricity and chemical affinity, in the forms of animals and plants, in the perceptions of the mind. Indeed, the direction of natural and physical science is towards a generalisation which shall express the fundamental laws of all by one simple numerical ratio. The mysticism of Pythagoras was vague only to the unlettered. It was a system of philosophy founded on existing mathematics which comprised more of the philosophy of numbers than our present."

Philosophical students of human nature have taken note of the danger professional and business men encounter when they extend their mental activities beyond the hour of four p.m. (by the sun). Thousands fail because of their ignorance of the fundamental laws governing all things physical. The morning hours up to ten a.m. are just as dangerous for many who are highly susceptible to the electric tension which occurs up to that hour. The feeling that prevails from four to eight in the afternoon is one of mental or physical fatigue, that in the morning one of irritability.

Lincoln was not immune from natural law. On one occasion, at five p.m., he was suddenly informed of the defeat of the Northern Forces, and it was feared by those who were present that he would fall to the ground. Mr. C. C. Coffin sprang forward to assist the President, who, however, succeeded in returning to the White House unaided.

Nature creates the natural, man the unnatural. Solomon declared: "To everything there is a season, and a time to every purpose."

Lincoln's Face

Knowledge, conviction, and certainty gave to Lincoln's face that penetrating power which could not have been assumed on occasion even by the most versatile and gifted actor.

The two following quotations from "The Valley of Shadows" describe Lincoln's personal appearance and the emotions produced by the expression of his features:—

"'The sperrit air more in the eye than it air in the tongue,' said Elihu Gest, rising from his seat; 'if Abe Lincoln looked at the wust slave-driver long enough Satan would give up every time.'

"'I see right away the difference a-twixt Lincoln en Douglas warn't so much in Lincoln bein' a good ways over six foot en Douglas a good ways under, ez it war in their eyes. The Jedge looked like he war speakin' agin time, but Abe Lincoln looked plumb through the meetin' into the everlastin'—the way Moses must hev looked when he see Canaan ahead—en I kin tell ye I never did see a man look that a-way.'"

Francis Grierson

The Great Debate

The hour had struck for the supreme test between the forces of slavery, on one hand, and the forces of freedom, on the other. A vast throng gathered at Alton from every section of the country to hear the last public discussion between the two antagonists, Lincoln and Douglas, and from the surging sea of faces thousands of anxious eyes gazed upward at the group of politicians on the balcony like wrecked mariners scanning the horizon for the smallest sign of a white sail of hope.

"This final debate resembled a duel between two men-of-war, the pick of a great fleet, all but these two sunk or abandoned in other waters, facing each other in the open, Douglas, the Little Giant, hurling at his opponent from his flagship of slavery his deadliest missiles, Lincoln calmly waiting to sink his antagonist by one single broadsider.

"Regarded in the light of spiritual reality, Lincoln and Douglas were predestined to meet side by side in this discussion, and it is hardly possible to give an adequate idea of the startling difference between the two temperaments: Douglas—short, plump, and petulant; Lincoln—long, gaunt, and self-possessed; the one white-haired and florid, the other black-haired and swarthy; the one educated and polished, the other unlettered and primitive.

"Judge Douglas opened the debate in a sonorous voice plainly heard by all, and with a look of mingled defiance and confidence he marshalled his facts and deduced his arguments. To the vigour of his attack there was added the prestige of the Senate Chamber, and it looked as if he would carry the majority with him. When, after a brilliant oratorical effort, he brought his speech to a close, it was amidst the shouts and yells of thousands of admirers.

"And now, Abraham Lincoln, the man who in 1830 undertook to split for Mrs. Nancy Miller four hundred rails for every yard of jean dyed with walnut bark that would be required to make him a pair of trousers, the flat-boatman, local stump-orator, and country lawyer, rose from his seat, stretched his long bony limbs upward, as if to get them in working order, and stood like some solitary pine on a lonely summit, very tall, very dark, very gaunt, and very rugged, his swarthy features stamped with a sad serenity, and the instant he began to speak the mouth lost its heaviness, the eyes attained a wondrous illumination, and the people stood bewildered and breathless under the natural magic of the most original personality known to the English-speaking world since Robert Burns.

"Every movement of his long muscular frame denoted inflexible earnestness, and a something issued forth, elemental and mystical, that told what the man had been, what he was, and what he would do in the future. Every look of the deep-set eyes, every movement of the prominent jaw, every wave of the brawny hand produced an impression, and before he had spoken twenty minutes the conviction took possession of thousands that here was the prophetic man of the present and the political saviour of the future."

Thus we see how Lincoln influenced persons, groups, crowds, whether he was sitting or standing, arguing or talking, rendering an opinion or listening to counsel.

Forecasting and Premonitions

Nothing great comes into the world unattended. Abraham Lincoln was surrounded by men and women who were predestined to their task without being fully aware of what they were doing. One of the most memorable mystical demonstrations ever recorded in any epoch occurred in the little town of Salem, Illinois, in August, 1837, when Lincoln was only twenty-three years of age, long before he had cut any figure in the political world. Accompanied by six lawyers and two doctors, Lincoln went from Springfield to Salem in a bandwagon to attend a camp-meeting. On the way Lincoln cracked jokes about the horses, the wagon, the lawyers, and many other things. When they arrived at the camp they found Doctor Peter Akers, one of the greatest Methodist preachers of the time, was about to preach a sermon on "The Dominion of Christ." The famous preacher declared that the Dominion of Christ could not come in America until slavery was destroyed. His sermon lasted three hours and he showed that a great civil war would put an end to human bondage.

"I am not a prophet," he said, "but a student of the Prophets; American slavery will come to an end in some near decade, I think in the sixties." These words caused a profound sensation. In their excitement thousands surged about the preacher, but when at last he cried out: "Who can tell but that the man who shall lead us through this strife may be standing in this presence," a solemn stillness fell over the assembly. There, not more than thirty feet away, stood the lank figure of Lincoln, with his pensive face, a prophet as yet uninspired, a leader as yet unannounced. The preacher's words had fallen like a mystical baptism on the head of this obscure pioneer, as yet unanointed by the sacrificial fire of the coming national tragedy.

When they returned to Springfield Lincoln remained silent for a long time. At last one of his friends asked him what he thought of the sermon and he replied that he "little dreamed that such power could be given to mortal man, for those words were from beyond the speaker. Peter Akers has convinced me that American slavery will go down with the crash of civil war." Then he added: "Gentlemen, you may be surprised and think it strange, but when the preacher was describing the civil war I distinctly saw myself, as in second sight, bearing an important part in that strife."

The next morning Mr. Lincoln came very late to his office, and Mr. Herndon, glancing at his haggard face, exclaimed: "Why, Lincoln, what's the matter?" Then Lincoln told him about the great sermon and said: "I am utterly unable to shake myself free from the conviction that I shall be involved in that terrible war."

Illumination of the Spirit

When Lincoln, young and unknown, visited New Orleans as a flat-boatman and saw men and women being sold at auction in the public mart, he said to the friend who was with him: "If ever I get a chance to hit that thing I'll hit it hard."

Who was this young man, whose clothes were in tatters, who was without patrons, to suggest such a thing as a chance to strike even a feeble blow at the institution of slavery? Dr. Gregg, commenting on this memorable incident, asks:

"Why did Lincoln utter these words? Was it an illumination of the Spirit forecasting the Civil War? Was it a whisper by a divine messenger that he was to be the chosen one to wipe the thing from the earth and give deliverance to millions of his fellow men?"

Few, if any, of Lincoln's biographers have touched on his early life with more than a superficial notion of its significance. Judge Whitney, in spite of his great knowledge and his deep insight, divides Lincoln's life into two parts, the first being uninspired, the second supernaturally wonderful. The truth is that the first part of his life contained a clear forecast of the second. Lincoln at the age of fifty-five was the same man, unchanged, excepting by experience. Only in fairy stories are people changed from fools into philosophers.

As a boy Lincoln was unlike any other boy, always unique, self-centred in the best and highest sense, the like of whom did not exist in his or any other country. All through his early life there could be seen the signs and symbols of his coming power. How such a being came into the world science fails to explain. Back of the mystery there are other mysteries, and not in a thousand years of experiment will eugenics produce another such mortal, not in ten thousand years will science create anything spiritual or mystical. Science can never get beyond the material. If it ever controls the psychic intelligence, mediocrity will be the order of the day. The higher intelligence does not need control but development. This freedom Lincoln had, but back of that apparent freedom the mystical conditions existed, fixed and foreordained. The very men and women who assisted him had to be where he found them. To have been anywhere else they would have been out of their proper element. In the human world there are no misfits, only grades of development.

Tycho Brahe and Lincoln

When Hugh Miller, the noted geologist, faced the inexplicable he committed suicide. But Tycho Brahe, the Danish astronomer, the greatest practical mystic the world of science has known, experienced a sense of joy and exhilaration every time he viewed the starry heavens through his telescope. He considered astronomy something "divine." His was the joyful pride of the seer who revels in the unexplained mysteries of the universe, and from time to time obtained clairvoyant glimpses of the working of the miracle. Brahe, like Abraham Lincoln, had moments when he perceived the inevitable with unalloyed vision.

After carefully studying the comet of 1577 he declared that it announced the birth of a prince in Finland who should lay waste Germany and vanish in 1632. Gustave Adolphus was born in Finland, overran Germany, and died in 1632.

Brahe was the forerunner of the true scientist, Lincoln the forerunner of the true statesman. It is not a fact that science and intuition are antagonistic. The antagonism exists only in the imagination of second-rate thinkers. The great discoverers always put the spiritual and the mystical above learning. Brahe and Newton, as scientists, were unequalled in their age and have not been surpassed in this. The Kultur of modern Germany has but emphasised the danger of pseudo science in all walks of life and made it plain that no nation can prosper under such an illusion. The Prussians have forced many to revert back to a consideration of the gifts of such men as Tycho Brahe, Newton, Lincoln, and the difference between their science and that of Kultur is a difference that strikes the normal thinker with amazement.

The true scientist is a seer who discloses new facts and discovers hidden laws. The true scientific mystic creates, but the votaries of Kultur destroy without creating. Yet, they will be destroyed by their own weapons. Modern materialism will go down under the weight of the material. The denial of the mystical forces of the universe is the vulnerable spot in the scientific armour of Krupp-Kultur. Let any one who wishes to be convinced by crude facts alone read the history of Frederick, the so-called Great, and then read a history of Lincoln. Then let the student ask which is the greater nation to-day—Prussia, headed by Frederick's descendant, or America, represented by Woodrow Wilson, the legitimate outcome of Washington the inspired patriot, and Lincoln the inspired emancipator?

Herndon's Analysis and Testimony

W. H. Herndon, for more than twenty years the law partner of Mr. Lincoln, delivered an address in Springfield, Illinois, upon the life and character of the lamented President, which for subtle analysis has few equals in biographical literature. The following are excerpts:

"Mr. Lincoln's perceptions were slow, cold, and exact. Everything came to him in its precise shape and colour. To some men the world of matter and of man comes ornamented with beauty, life, and action, and hence more or less false and inexact. No lurking illusion or other error, false in itself, and clad for the moment in robes of splendour, ever passed undetected or unchallenged over the threshold of his mind—that point that divides vision from the realm and home of thought."

"Names to him were nothing, and titles naught—assumption always standing back abashed at his cold, intellectual glare. Neither his perceptions nor intellectual vision were perverted, distorted, or diseased. He saw all things through a perfect, mental lens. There was no diffraction or refraction there. He was not impulsive, fanciful, or imaginative, but calm and precise. He threw his whole mental light around the object, and, in time, substance and quality stood apart; form and colour took their appropriate places, and all was clear and exact in his mind. In his mental view he crushed the unreal, the inexact, the hollow, and the sham.... To some minds the world is all life, a soul beneath the material; but to Mr. Lincoln no life was individual or universal that did not manifest itself to him. His mind was his standard. His perceptions were cool, persistent, pitiless in pursuit of the truth. No error went undetected and no falsehood unexposed if he once was aroused in search of truth.

An Original Mind

"Mr. Lincoln saw philosophy in a story and a schoolmaster in a joke. No man saw nature, fact, thing, from his standpoint. His was a new and original position, which was always suggesting, hinting something to him. Nature, insinuations, hints, and suggestions were new, fresh, original, and odd to him. The world, fact, man, principle, all had their powers of suggestion to his susceptible soul. They continually put him in mind of something known or unknown. Hence his power and tenacity of what is called association of ideas. His susceptibilities to all suggestions and hints enabled him at will to call up readily the associated and classified fact and idea.

"Mr. Lincoln was often at a loss for a word and hence was compelled to resort to stories, and maxims, and jokes to embody his idea, that it might be comprehended. So true was this peculiar mental vision of his, that though mankind has been gathering, arranging, and classifying facts for thousands of years, Lincoln's peculiar standpoint could give him no advantage of other men's labour. Hence he tore up to the deep foundations all arrangements of facts, and coined and arranged new plans to govern himself. His labour was great, continuous, patient, and all-enduring.

The Great Books

"The truth about the whole matter is that Mr. Lincoln read less and thought more than any man in his sphere in America. When young he read the Bible, and when of age he read Shakespeare. The latter book was scarcely ever out of his mind. Mr. Lincoln is acknowledged to have been a great man, but the question is, what made him great? I repeat, that he read less and thought more than any man of his standing in America, if not in the world. He possessed originality and power of thought in an eminent degree. He was cautious, cool, patient, and enduring. These are some of the grounds of his wonderful success. Not only was nature, man, fact, and principle suggestive to Mr. Lincoln, not only had he accurate and exact perceptions, but he was causative, i. e., his mind ran back behind all facts, things, and principles to their origin, history, and first cause—to that point where forces act at once as effect and cause. He would stop and pause in the street and analyse a machine. He would whittle things to a point and then count the numberless inclined planes, and their pitch, making the point. Mastering and defining this, he would then cut that point back, and get a broad transverse section of his pine stick, and peel and define that. Clocks, omnibuses, language, paddle-wheels, and idioms never escaped his observation and analysis. Before he could form any idea of anything, before he would express his opinion on any subject, he must know its origin and history, in substance and quality, in magnitude and gravity. He must know his subject inside and outside, upside and downside.

"He searched his own mind and nature thoroughly, as I have often heard him say. He must analyse a sensation, an idea, and words, and run them back to their origin, history, purpose, and destiny. He was most emphatically a merciless analyser of facts, things, and principles. When all these processes had been well and thoroughly gone through, he could form an opinion and express it, but no sooner. Hence when he did speak his utterances rang out gold-like, quick, keen, and current upon the counters of the understanding. He reasoned logically, through analogy and comparison. All opponents dreaded him in his originality of idea, condensation, definition, and force of expression, and wo be to the man who hugged to his bosom a secret error if Mr. Lincoln got on the chase of it. I say, wo to him! Time could hide the error in no nook or corner of space in which he would not detect and expose it.

Veneration and Truth

"The predominating elements of Mr. Lincoln's peculiar character, were: firstly, his great capacity and powers of reason; secondly, his excellent understanding; thirdly, an exalted idea of the sense of right and equity; and fourthly, his intense veneration of what was true and good. His reason ruled all other faculties of his mind.

"His pursuit of truth was indefatigable, terrible. He reasoned from his well-chosen principles with such clearness, force, and compactness that the tallest intellects in the land bowed to him in this respect.

"He came down from his throne of logic with irresistible and crushing force. His printed speeches prove this, but his speeches before the Supreme Courts of the State and Nation would demonstrate it.

"Mr. Lincoln was an odd and original man; he lived by himself and out of himself. He was a very sensitive man, unobtrusive and gentlemanly, and often hid himself in the common mass of men in order to prevent the discovery of his individuality. He had no insulting egotism and no pompous pride; no haughtiness. He was not an upstart and had no insolence. He was a meek, quiet, unobtrusive gentleman.

"Not only were Mr. Lincoln's perceptions good; not only was nature suggestive to him; not only was he original and strong; not only had he great reason and understanding; not only did he love the true and good; not only was he tender and kind—but, in due proportion, he had a glorious combination of them all.

"He had no avarice in his nature or other like vice. He did not care who succeeded to the presidency of this or that Christian Association or Railroad Convention; who made the most money; who was going to Philadelphia, when and for what, and what were the costs of such a trip. He could not understand why men struggled for such things as these.

The Great Puzzle

"One day, at Washington, he made this remark to me: 'If ever this free people, if this Government itself is ever utterly demoralised, it will come from this human wriggle and struggle for office—a way to live without work.'

"It puzzled him at Washington to know and to get at the root of this dread desire, this contagious disease of national robbery in the nation's death-struggle.

"This man, this long, bony, wiry, sad man, floated into our country in 1831, in a frail canoe, down the north fork of the Sangamon River, friendless, penniless, powerless, and alone—begging for work in our city—ragged, struggling for the common necessities of life. This man, this peculiar man, left us in 1861, the President of the United States, backed by friends, power, fame, and all human force."

Lincoln's Energy and Will

Energy is usually a blind force in the conduct of human affairs and the greatest with which we have to deal. History is made up of the deeds of individuals with a surplus of energy, which overflows and damages governments as floods damage lands.

Will, energy, and ambition are, in most cases, synonymous terms. Without energy the will breaks down, and without ambition energy and will would prove innocuous. No one can doubt that misdirected energy was at the bottom of much that moved the Prussians and that their ambitions were wholly material, limited to geographical boundaries. Lincoln displayed physical as well as mental energy in a supernormal degree; his will was as fixed as a mountain of adamant, while his ambition was not personal, but national and universal. Only the practical mystic could direct such forces with wisdom, and as we look still closer into the mystery of his temperament the question of pride and vanity arises, and their relation to ambition and will.

In the first place, what causes ambition? Pride, answers the world. But the world is wrong. Ambition is not the result of pride but of vanity. Solomon, the wisest and greatest man of his time, was a proud man and a wise ruler until he began to import apes and peacocks. Then vanity usurped the place of pride and he came to the end of his temporal tether.

Vanity caused Napoleon to have himself crowned Emperor of the French, and from that day his power declined. A proper sense of pride would have led him to stop where he was and refuse all further manifestations and developments of worldly honour. Pride tends to moral dignity and intellectual reticence, and that is why Lincoln blushed in the presence of the institution of slavery. His pride gave him an acute sense of shame and his honour an acute sense of justice. Only the vain will consent to live in idleness while others slave for them. Vanity induces anything from the ridiculous to the criminal, and those controlled by it are subject to absurd statements and ridiculous actions. They cannot avoid both. Washington and Lincoln were free from the fetters of ridicule. They were imbued with a subconscious pride which stood for the whole nation.

Nature and Prophecy

Herndon says:—

"I cannot refrain from noting the views Lincoln held in reference to the great questions of moral and social reforms under which he classed suffrage for women, temperance, and slavery. 'All such questions, he observed one day, as we were discussing temperance in the office, 'must find lodgment with the most enlightened souls who stamp them with their approval. In God's own time they will be organised into law and woven into the fabric of all our institutions.'"

As the Divine principle permeates all nature, so Lincoln, being a pure product of nature, possessed the secret consciousness of natural power, illumined by mystical intuition and guided by the higher forces of the spirit. He realised the superiority of mind over matter, of intelligence over ignorance, of wisdom over learning, of illumination over mere knowledge. He was another Marcus Aurelius, without the influence of paganism, free from the trammels of mythology. He inquired into the mystery of his own being and delved into the darkest corners of personality and character. Some of his deepest thoughts on the mysteries of life and death were never voiced by this man who never spoke unless he deemed it imperative to speak.

Lincoln, indeed, never gossipped about people and books. He was not a gossip. His jokes were for a purpose, his talk was for a purpose, and his meditations were fundamental.

The Seal of Nature

Herndon was right when he said that Lincoln's features were stamped with the seal of nature. This is the only seal that is beyond imitation. All else can be mimicked. We have seen how ghastly one or two persons appeared when they attempted to look like Lincoln. The imitation took on the appearance of pale, dull putty. The notion that Lincoln's personality could be imitated with success was quite in keeping with that other notion that the great President was, in spite of everything, just one of the common people. But Lincoln as he appears in popular histories, and Lincoln as he was known to his associates and those who came into personal contact with him, are two different persons. Perhaps no one has summed up the matter with such concision and force as Don Piatt, who knew him well:—

"With all his awkwardness of manner and utter disregard of social conventionalities that seemed to invite familiarity, there was something about Abraham Lincoln that enforced respect. No man presumed on the apparent invitation to be other than respectful. I was told at Springfield that this accompanied him through life. Among his rough associates, when young, he was leader, looked up to and obeyed, because they felt of his muscle and its readiness in use. Among his associates at the bar it was attributed to his wit, which kept his duller associates at a distance. But the fact was that this power came from a sense of reserve force of intellectual ability that no one took account of save in its results. Through one of those manifestations of nature that produce a Shakespeare at long intervals, a giant had been born to the poor whites of Kentucky and the sense of superiority possessed Lincoln at all times. Seward, Chase, and Stanton, great as they were, felt their inferiority to their master."

Law and Authority

We are beginning to feel the reality of that power that lies above appearance and formula, that power manifested in Job and Isaiah, which we accept as inspiration in religion, intuition in philosophy, and illumination in art, producing saints in one age and mystical scientists in another.

We float through the ether on a revolving miracle called the earth, returning again and again to attain the same figure on the dial of time. The things done by human automatons count for nothing in the course of destiny.

We think we are wise when we invent a new name for an old truth; and vanity aims to confine the infinite within the limits of a stopper bottle or a glass showcase, or attain inspiration by means of a ouija board.

Can any one conceive what would have happened to this country had Lincoln made use of such a contrivance to direct the course of his actions? This scourge of dead agnostics seems like an ironical stroke of nature to discount their disbelief. Not only does this clumsy instrument make wits like Mark Twain "talk like poor Pol," but it makes philosophers reason like first-grade pupils at our common schools.

Immortality is destined to have the last word even though it be pronounced in the most fantastic manner.

Lincoln believed in law, order, and authority. He believed in the mission of the churches. He was a regular worshipper in Dr. Gurley's Presbyterian congregation at the Capital. He was a praying president, like George Washington, and, while he was not a member of any church, he was convinced that all the churches were necessary. He was not a free-thinker, as that term is commonly used. Loose reasoning and vague, uncertain doctrines he could not abide. He demanded proofs and would not accept a man's word merely from sentimental motives. No one ever induced him to "side-track" from the main line of argument and reason. His attitude in the matter of inspiration and spiritual direction may be summed up in a few words spoken at the time a delegation of Chicago ministers came to him, urging him in God's name to free the slaves without further delay. His reply was that when the Almighty wanted him to free the slaves He would deal directly with Lincoln himself instead of indirectly through Chicago.

A vacillating President would have been influenced by such a request at such a time, but the President had faith in his own illuminations and awaited orders from a Supreme source. Had he been influenced by advice given by all sorts of people who called at the White House on all sorts of missions, possessing no authority themselves, what turmoil and chaos would have resulted to the army and the Nation!

Practical mystic that he was, he did not seek, nor wish for, advice from people in matters which concerned his own judgment alone. It is true that on several occasions he was approached by persons who came with messages of various kinds assumed to be spiritual, but Lincoln received them with a neutral politeness, sometimes mingled with a grim humour, as when Robert Dale Owen read to him a long manuscript presumed to be highly inspirational and illuminating, and Lincoln replied, "Well, for those who like that sort of thing that is the thing they would like."

Lincoln as Critic

Nothing escaped Lincoln's powers of philosophical and metaphysical analysis. He did not read the Bible and Shakespeare merely for pleasure, as people read novels. He could give excellent reasons for everything he did. Even in his most listless moods he never lost his firm grip on affairs, both general and individual. When he read a book it was because there was something in it which helped him to penetrate deeper into the recesses of life and character. He would study a passage or a chapter until he had assimilated its wisdom and its mystical import.

Lincoln was a natural critic. When Walt Whitman's "Leaves O' Grass" was first published a copy of the book was read and discussed by several of his friends in Springfield. Lincoln at once recognised the fact that a new poetic genius had appeared and he did not permit adverse opinions to influence his judgment. He cared nothing for the romantic in itself. He cared only for those phases of literature which induce serious philosophical or spiritual thought. While his partner read Carlyle, he read Shakespeare.

In the Spring of 1862 the President spent several days at Fortress Monroe awaiting military operations upon the

Peninsula. As a portion of the Cabinet were with him, that was temporarily the seat of government, and he bore with him constantly the burden of public affairs. His favourite diversion was reading Shakespeare. One day—it chanced to be the day before the capture of Norfolk—as he sat reading alone, he called to his side Colonel Le Grand B. Cannon. "You have been writing long enough, Colonel," he said, "come in here; I want to read you a passage in Hamlet." He read the discussion on ambition between Hamlet and his courtiers, and the soliloquy in which conscience debates of a future state.

His Style

"No criticism of Mr. Lincoln," says the Spectator, "can be in any sense adequate which does not deal with his astonishing power over words. It is not too much to say of him that he is among the greatest masters of prose ever produced by the English race. Self-educated, or rather not educated at all in the ordinary sense, he contrived to obtain an insight and power in the handling and mechanism of letters such as has been given to but few men in his, or, indeed, in any age. That the gift of oratory should be a natural gift is understandable enough, for the methods of the orator, like those of the poet, are primarily sensuous and may well be instinctive.... Mr. Lincoln did not get his ability to handle prose through his gift of speech. It is in his conduct of the pedestrian portions of composition that Mr. Lincoln's genius for prose style is exhibited." Lincoln avoided the superfluous in writing as in speaking, and style came after the matter of his thought, not as a conscious effort while he was uttering his thoughts. He was not consciously a literary artist. When, in his famous inaugural address, he made "pray" rhyme with "away," it sounded like a false note struck in the movement of a great symphony. That blemish remains like a flaw in a diamond which cannot be removed, but the miracle remains that this master of men and moods accomplished in his speeches and letters what no one else accomplished in his time.

Lincoln's Serenity

"Lincoln," says the same writer in the Spectator, "saw things as a disillusioned man sees them, and yet, in the bad sense, he never suffered any disillusionment. For suffusing and combining his other qualities was a serenity of mind which affected the whole man. He viewed the world too much as a whole to be greatly troubled or perplexed over its accidents. To this serenity of mind was due an almost total absence of indignation in the ordinary sense."

This is true, because, as Walt Whitman says, "The foundations of his character, more than any man's in history, were mystic and spiritual."

"Lincoln was, before all things, a gentleman," says the Spectator, "and the good taste inseparable from that character made it impossible for him to be spoiled by power and position. This grace and strength of character is never better shown than in the letters to his generals, victorious or defeated. If a general had to be reprimanded he did it as only the most perfect gentleman could do it."

Nevertheless, the invulnerable President did show his anger or indignation on some few occasions. And justly so. As a rule he did not consider it worth his while to permit himself to be moved by the sayings and doings of any one. The foolish are unworthy of indignation; they must be dealt with quietly but effectively; while the others must be managed with gentle firmness backed by the fundamentally drastic. Fuss and fury were unknown to this pioneer politician, philosophical statesman, and mystical leader.

No man can be serene who doubts himself. Lincoln, when in doubt as to the actions of others, did not grope in the darkness, but waited. His invincible trust in Providence held him aloof from the petty circumstances and daily routine of intrigue, and his imagination soared in the empyrean while those around him flattered themselves that he was being influenced or led by their counsels and their interests.

He treated people who bedevilled him with importunities and all sorts of advice as the wise parent treats a child who asks for the impossible—he knew that a little waiting would wear them out and they would end by forgetting. Often, in place of a flat refusal, he would turn away the office-seeker by a sudden, adroit stroke of his humour, thus sending the man and his friends away smiling good-humouredly at Lincoln's inimitable tact.

The Romance of His Character

There is a "romance of character" that accompanies people of exceptional achievements, as Emerson has so justly said, and Lincoln possessed it without being in the slightest degree conscious of the fact. This is one reason why his life surpasses in interest any book of fiction ever written. He united all the realism of pioneer life with the romance of the inexplicable and the fascination of the unexpected.

Those who come to Lincoln in search of the shifting romance of bohemianism will be disappointed, for the romance of change and vacillation is the kind that leads to the poorhouse or the hospital. This romance of character, belonging, as it did, to the temperament of the man, was hidden from the multitude, but all could readily see the romance of the progressive events of his life. Lincoln was at times awed, but not alarmed, by the turn of affairs which placed him at the head of the nation. He realised the tremendous responsibility without regrets or fear. He was fully conscious of his mission but quite unconscious of the romantic elements which enveloped it, for Lincoln's life included both the "romance of character" and the romance of experience. Without the first, the second would have unfitted him for the heavy responsibilities of his high office later on. He did not seek experience for the sake of experience, like so many in our day who are under the illusion that truth and wisdom arrive perforce. He forced nothing. He followed a natural course of events, dealing with each according to the light of his own judgment, asking for no advice.

Neither the romance of character nor the romance of experience comes to those who seek them. Self-consciousness dissipates romantic mystery.

President by the Grace of God

Lincoln lived long enough to become convinced that everything exists for a purpose. He saw that the Rebellion had to be, and that in the seeming confusion of sentiments and interests the Divine ruled over all persons and parties.

Events had to follow as ordained by the spiritual Power that lies behind appearance. Lincoln worked in the light; Czar Nicholas of Russia lived in the dark. He could not tell why he occupied the Russian throne. Lincoln knew why he occupied the White House. The Kaiser was not able to see why will, energy, and money should not rule the world.

Never were the lessons taught by Lincoln's career so much needed as now, when a ruthless autocracy is seeking to get rid of all moral responsibility, while, on the other hand, thousands are awakening to the necessity of a new order, of fostering the mystical renaissance.

Francis Grierson

Science and the Mystical

Quintilian said:—

"No man can become a perfect orator without a knowledge of geometry. It is not without reason that the greatest men have bestowed extreme attention on this science."

Locke, the philosopher, gives the reason:—

"Geometry develops the habit of pursuing long trains of ideas which will remain with the student who will be enabled to pierce through the mazes of sophism and discover a latent truth, when persons who have not this habit will never find it."

Lincoln was passionately fond of geometry. His oratory was based on logic, but his logic came from the mystical absolute, a geometric science of the soul which he alone could appropriate through his perception of fundamental principles of universal law. He could perceive that an idea is a personal conception of a mathematical truth, as distinguished from mere beliefs, notions, and sentiments. Others turned politics into the art of influencing crowds through their sentimental opinions; Lincoln engaged in trying to make them think logically. While others gave vague reasons for their political views he gave reasons based on law which he explained with simple force and lucid phraseology.

He never attempted to tell all he knew. The practical mystic never does. He knew how he acquired his knowledge, but his reticence was as pronounced as his gift of expression. It was this quality of reticence that kept him from taking counsel from all sorts of statesmen and explaining the inexplicable. There was not a man among them that could have understood. In this, Lincoln was a mystic, full-fledged, initiated, as by centuries of experience. His innate wisdom told him exactly how much the people could understand, how much politicians could digest, and how much statesmen could divine. Not only did he hold the allegiance of the Whigs, but he gained the allegiance of the Abolitionists. This, indeed, was intellect illumined.

The Old and the New

How old yet new are nature's moods and manifestations! How mysteriously the souvenirs of the past are revived and quickened in new forms, faces, and phenomena! The seasons come and go with varying moods and seem new, but they are older than the formulas of civilisation; strangers bring with them new influences, but we discover in them something familiar from the vague and shadowy past. Every single thing is related to every other thing, and illuminated minds are the periods that separate the cycles, but not the laws, of human progress. The form is new; the principle remains unchangeable. Solomon was unique in his glory, but Athens had a Pericles, Rome a Cæsar, Europe a Bonaparte, and the new world a Lincoln.

Real genius is elemental. It influences humanity as much as heat and cold, rain and sunshine. People who offer the greatest opposition to it are those who fall before its onward march. Indeed, it seems to be, from all historical accounts, a sort of car of Juggernaut to those who wilfully oppose it. And this is not surprising since it is the greatest power of which man has any personal knowledge, supported by all the forces of the material and the spiritual.

Destiny versus Will

Great men float into power on mystical waves moved by the force of destiny. The greater the mind the greater the fixture of force behind it.

Between George Washington and Abraham Lincoln, Presidents came and went as figureheads of parties or props to some ephemeral political scaffold. The majority were stopgaps. They, like the majority of politicians and many others, put their trust in Will and Desire. They could not understand that a man is not great because of his will, but because of his innate knowledge. Washington realised his destiny and understood. Lincoln realised what he was and what he would become long before his nomination for the Presidency, but he was wholly unconscious of any Will to Power. The born statesman is aware of his invincible, hidden knowledge, and he places Will in the second rank. He knows it counts for nothing in the fundamental issues.

Lincoln discerned, at an early age, the difference between desire and destiny. He saw the dangerous illusions under which the Will-to-Power-politicians and others laboured and how vain were their hopes.

Will and Ambition are characteristics of men who mistake the material for the permanent. Bonaparte and Bismarck exercised their Will for the possession of the material and both failed. The Hohenzollerns and their henchmen have failed in the same exercise. This exercise is indulged in by people who believe that to become intensely individualistic means the development of powerful personality. They talk of their rights as if their desires gave them the privilege of robbing their neighbours. And what some are doing publicly others are doing privately.

The motives for this desire for material domination vary with the individual. With one, it is to get even with a group; with another, it is to get even with a party; with others, it is to appear in public, to be frequently named and sometimes applauded. Compromise and subterfuge are ingredients inseparable from the illusions of the Will. While Lincoln often assisted his friends, he refused to hedge or trim in order to please. Destiny behind him was invulnerable, his own sense of justice inexorable. While others were working for the good of their city, state, or section, he was thinking of the good of the whole country, with all humanity behind it. Destiny created the man and the crisis at the same time, as always happens. The one could not exist without the other. Destiny is the collective conscience acting through elective genius. For this reason Lincoln was not only the man of his time but the man whose example will exert the greatest influence on future eras.

James Jacquess Practical Mystic

In the hubbub and confusion created by the upheaval which began in 1914 it is of vital importance for thinking people of the English-speaking countries to know what went on in the inner circles at Washington during that year of trial, 1864, when the destiny of the Union seemed to be hanging in the balance. It is time to know the truth about Lincoln's supernaturalism. Your favourite historian avoids the subject. He will not touch on a matter so dangerous to his neutral agnosticism. He avoids the details of the supernatural events of that wonderful time. He will discuss anything but that; he knows that once thinking people become acquainted with the facts they will begin to form their own conclusions.

In Lincoln's day agnosticism had not taken root in the intellectual soil of this country. The negative writings of Darwin and Spencer were unknown among politicians and statesmen, and the churches still believed that "spirit" ruled matter and that Providence was directing the affairs of the nation.

In Lincoln's time agnostic ministers were unknown. All believed in a positive religion. The Union was saved from disruption because Lincoln and his aids were firm believers in a higher Power and a higher destiny. Doubt, cynicism, and scepticism would have handed the country over to universal chaos. The downfall of the Union would have meant the end of the British Empire and to-day Kaiserism would be in supreme command of the remnant of Anglo-Saxon civilisation.

It is the fashion to read romantic novels, but the story of the Jacquess peace mission is more fascinating than any novel because it is fact instead of fiction and because its basic element is the supernatural.

James Jacquess was, himself, a practical mystic of no uncertain power but whose great gifts were overshadowed by the personality of Lincoln, his revered chief. Before the Civil War Jacquess was a mathematician, a Greek and Latin scholar, a college president, and one of the most forcible Methodist preachers of the age. His field of work was the country around Springfield, where Lincoln often heard him preach. Long before Jacquess received the mystical command to undertake his peace mission to the Rebel headquarters at Richmond, Lincoln knew and respected him as a sincere and earnest patriot. Jacquess was Colonel of an Illinois regiment during the war, and had already taken a valiant part in some of the most terrible battles.

Colonel Jacquess was inspired to act as he did without, at first, consulting any one. He conceived the idea of going to Richmond, interviewing the Confederate leaders, and so gaining some definite information that would eventually lead to peace, through victory, for the Union. His mission was a secret, known only to a limited circle, including the President, General Rosecrans, General Garfield (who later became President), and James R. Gilmore, the friend of Lincoln.

Mr. Gilmore, in his "Personal Recollections of Lincoln," devotes many pages to this peace mission, with all the details, from its inception by Colonel Jacquess to its final wonderful results.

General Garfield, writing to Mr. Gilmore from his military headquarters on June 17th, 1863, said:—

"Colonel Jacquess has gone on his peace mission. The President approved it, though, of course, he did not make it an official matter. There are some very curious facts relating to his mission which I hope to tell you some day. It will be sufficient for me to say that enough of the mysterious is in it to give me an almost superstitious feeling of faith, and certainly a great interest, in his work. He is most solemnly in earnest and has great confidence in his mission."

Colonel Jacquess succeeded in gaining a respectful hearing before the highest authorities at Richmond without being shot as a spy—more than one of his friends having predicted such a fate for him.

He returned to the North determined to await patiently for another opportunity to try again. In 1864, after conferring with Mr. Gilmore and the President, it was decided that a second mission should be set on foot, this time in company with his friend Gilmore, whom a special Providence had chosen to record all the incidents and events of that unprecedented undertaking.

On this occasion Colonel Jacquess learned all that he had hoped to learn, and more, from the lips of Jefferson Davis, President of the Southern Confederacy; and when Jacquess and Gilmore returned Lincoln requested Mr. Gilmore to prepare a detailed account of the astounding revelation for the Atlantic Monthly.

This vivid recital of the facts was published and it created a sensation from one end of the country to the other. It turned the tide in favour of Lincoln's election for a second term and saved the Union. This, in brief, was the work of Jacquess, the mystic, whose name to-day is only known to the more serious students of Lincoln's life and work. Had the President been less a practical mystic than he was he would have forbidden Colonel Jacquess to undertake a journey full of risks and peril, and one that ordinary business men would have called an insane adventure.

Images and Dreams

Noah Brooks, in his Life of Lincoln, gives the following account of a vision which the President described to him:—

"It was just after my nomination in 1860 when the news was coming thick and fast all day, and there had been a great Hurrah Boys, so that I was well tired out, and went home to rest and threw myself on a lounge in my chamber. Opposite where I lay was a bureau with a swinging glass, and looking in the glass I saw myself reflected, nearly at full length, but my face, I noticed, had two separate and distinct images, the tip of the nose of one being about three inches from the tip of the other. I was a little bothered, perhaps startled, and got up and looked in the glass, but the illusion vanished. On lying down again I saw it a second time, plainer, if possible, than before. Then I noticed that one of the faces was a little paler, say five shades, than the other. I got up and the thing melted away. I left, and in the excitement of the hour forgot all about it, nearly but not quite, for the thing would once in a while come up and give me a little pang, as though something uncomfortable had happened. Later in the day I told my wife about it, and a few days later I tried the experiment again, when, sure enough, the thing came again. My wife thought that it was a sign that I was to be elected to a second term of office and that the paleness of one of the faces was an omen that I should not live through the last term."

Not long after his second inauguration he said to a friend in Washington:—

"I have seen this evening what I saw on the evening of my nomination. As I stood before a mirror I saw two images of myself—a bright one in front and one that was pallid, standing behind. It completely unnerved me. The bright one I know is my past, the pale one my coming life. I do not think I shall live to see the end of my second term."

In his biography, Morgan relates a dream which Lincoln had. He thought he was in a vast assembly, and the people drew back to let him pass. Just then Lincoln heard some one say: "He is a common-looking fellow." Lincoln, in his dream, turned to the man and said: "Friend, the Lord prefers common-looking people; that is the reason He makes so many of them."

Shortly before Lincoln's assassination some friends were talking about certain dreams recorded in the Bible when the President said:

"About two days ago I retired very late. I could not have been long in bed when I fell into a slumber, for I was weary. I soon began to dream. There seemed to be a deathlike stillness about me. Then I heard subdued sobs, as if a number of people were weeping. I thought I left my bed and wandered downstairs. There the silence was broken by the same pitiful sobbing, but the mourners were invisible. I went from room to room; no living person was in sight, but the same mournful sounds of distress met me as I passed along. It was light in all the rooms; every object was familiar to me, but where were all the people who were grieving as if their hearts would break? I was puzzled and alarmed. What could be the meaning of all this? Determined to find the cause of a state of things so mysterious and so shocking, I kept on until I arrived at the East Room, which I entered. Before me was a catafalque on which was a form wrapped in funeral vestments. Around it were stationed soldiers who were acting as guards; there was a throng of people, some gazing mournfully upon the catafalque; others weeping pitifully. 'Who is dead in the White House?' I demanded of one of the soldiers. 'The President,' was the answer. 'He was killed by an assassin.' Then came a loud burst of grief from the crowd, which woke me from my dream."

The New Era

The principles enunciated by Abraham Lincoln are abiding examples, not only for the English-speaking peoples but for the whole world.

Out of what seems universal confusion, tending towards chaos, there arises a new era. A material transformation had to occur before the uprising of the spiritual, and the truth is beginning to dawn in the minds of thousands that behind all material phenomena there dwells the divine idea. Before the gates of oblivion closed on civilisation we were plucked from the gulf in accordance with the Divine purpose.

Amidst the strife of contending factions the thunder of upheaval reverberates from continent to continent, heralding the close of a dispensation that has known the trials and triumphs of nearly two thousand years, from which is emerging the mystical dawn of a new day.

THE END

www.ingramcontent.com/pod-product-compliance
Lightning Source LLC
Chambersburg PA
CBHW020911080526
44589CB00011B/546